CREATION
Crafts

Darlene Hoffa

Illustrated by Bill Clark

CONCORDIA

Publishing House
St. Louis

Copyright © 1993 Concordia Publishing House
3558 S. Jefferson Avenue, St. Louis, MO 63118-3968
Manufactured in the United States of America

1   2   3   4   5   6   7   8   9   10   02   01   00   99   98   97   96   95   94   93

Contents

Be a Rainbow Keeper

God painted a rainbow in the sky as a reminder of His promise that He would never send a flood so large that it would cover all the earth. God loves all of His creatures and cares for them. God loves and cares for you.

Materials

Cotton balls
Crayons or markers
Scissors
Glue
Yarn

Directions

1. Color the rainbow as indicated.
2. Cut out the rainbow and glue three cotton balls at each end of the rainbow.
3. Draw or glue a picture of yourself in the center of the rainbow.
4. Punch a hole and tie a loop of yarn at the top of your rainbow.

1.
2.
3.
4.
5.
6.

Whenever the rainbow appears in the clouds, I will see it and remember the everlasting covenant between God and all living creatures of every kind on the earth.
Genesis 9:16

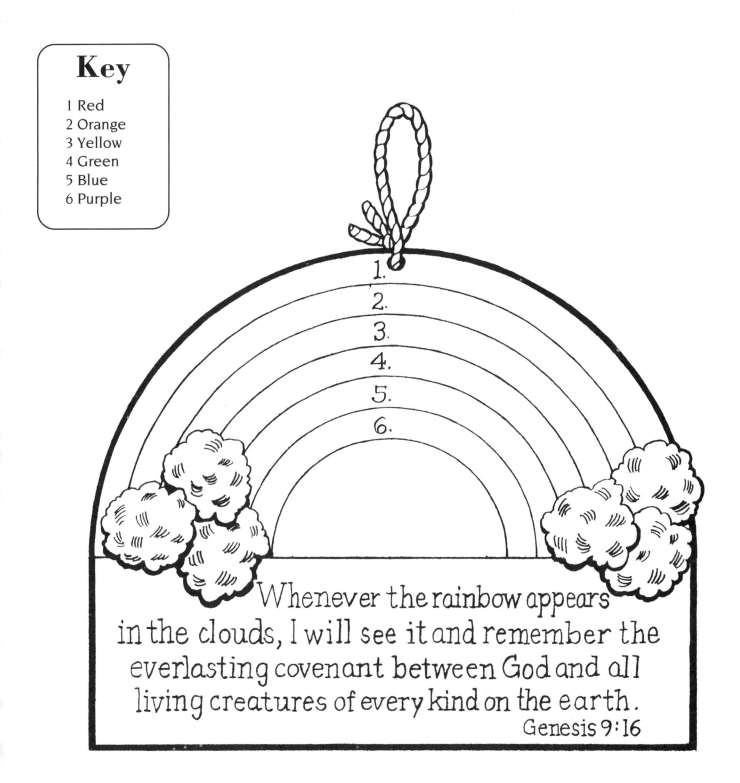

Key

1 Red
2 Orange
3 Yellow
4 Green
5 Blue
6 Purple

1.
2.
3.
4.
5.
6.

Whenever the rainbow appears in the clouds, I will see it and remember the everlasting covenant between God and all living creatures of every kind on the earth.
Genesis 9:16

Plant a Tree and Help It Grow

2

God made trees to give us cool shade and delicious fruit. He made them to add oxygen to the air for us to breathe. Plant a tree and water it carefully. Watch the tree grow and thank God for helping you grow in His love. Then make a paper tree to remind you of God's care.

Materials

Pencil
Green tissue paper cut into 1-inch squares
Red tissue paper cut into 1-inch squares
Brown tissue paper cut into 1-inch squares
Glue
Scissors
Cardboard

Directions

1. Copy pattern and glue to a piece of cardboard.
2. Place a 1-inch square of green tissue paper over the eraser end of the pencil.
3. Curl paper around end of pencil.
4. Use the pencil to dip curled paper in glue, then press onto leafy part of tree. (Young children can crumble tissue paper squares with fingers and glue to tree.)
5. Continue process, using red for the apples and brown for the trunk, until tree is completed.

Pattern 2: Plant a Tree and Help It Grow   © CPH 1993

Raise Some Vegetables

God made good food for you to eat. Plant a vegetable garden and grow food for meals and snacks. Then make a picture of a vegetable garden. Show it to your family at dinnertime and say a thank-You prayer to God for making good food.

Materials

Brown paper grocery sack
Crayons or markers
Construction paper
Scissors
Glue

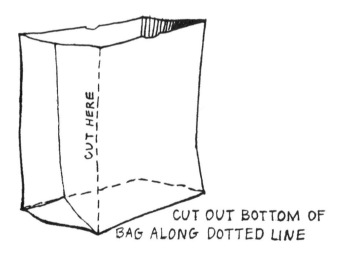

CUT HERE

CUT OUT BOTTOM OF BAG ALONG DOTTED LINE

Directions

1. Cut a piece of brown paper from a grocery sack.
2. Draw a line across the middle of the paper to indicate ground level.
3. Color the vegetables on the next page, or use them as patterns to make construction paper vegetables.
3. Cut out the vegetables.
4. Glue vegetables which grow above ground above the line. Glue vegetables which are roots under the line.
5. Use crayons, markers, or construction paper to add leaves, the sun, and a blue sky.

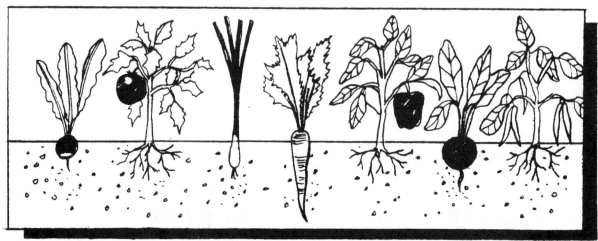

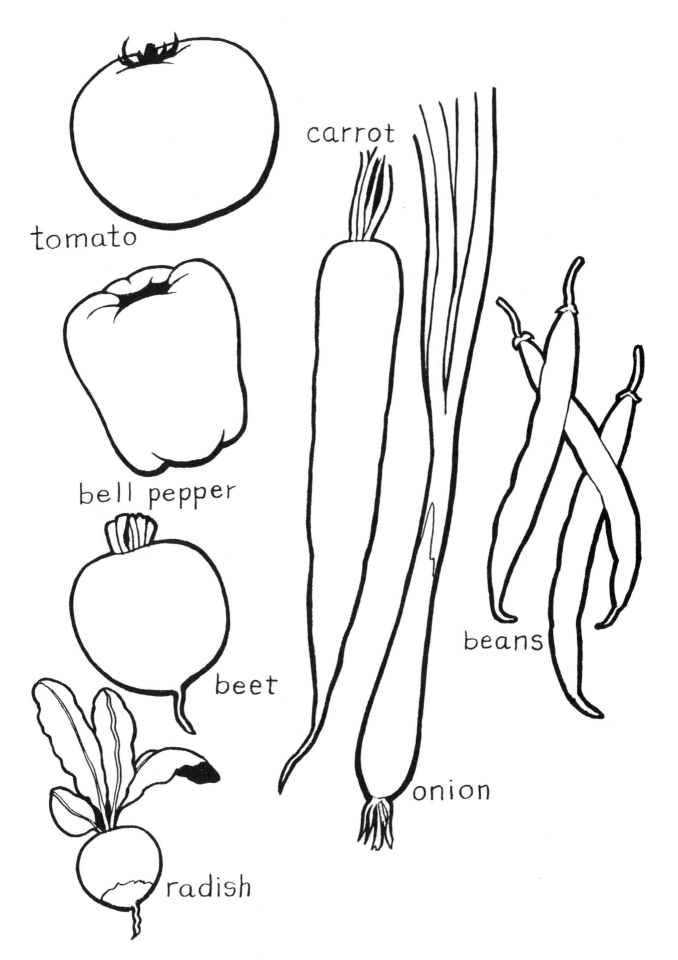

tomato

bell pepper

beet

radish

carrot

onion

beans

Pattern 3: Raise Some Vegetables © CPH 1993 **9**

Eat a Bowl of Soup

Enjoy eating a bowl of vegetable soup with your family. Take turns naming some of the good foods God gives you to enjoy. Then make a picture of vegetable soup.

Materials

Orange construction paper
Crayons or markers
Paper place mat or sheet of
    construction paper
Scissors
Glue

Directions

1. Use the inner circle on the next page as a pattern to cut a circle from orange paper.
2. Glue orange circle in center of larger circle.
3. Color vegetables, cut, and glue them on orange circle.
4. Glue the soup picture on a paper place mat or sheet of construction paper.
5. Color spoon, cut, and glue at side of bowl. (The soup picture can also be glued inside a 6-inch paper bowl.)

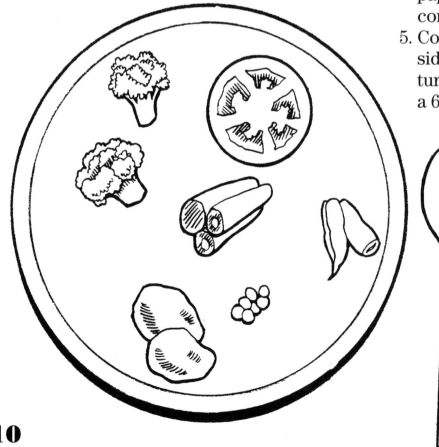

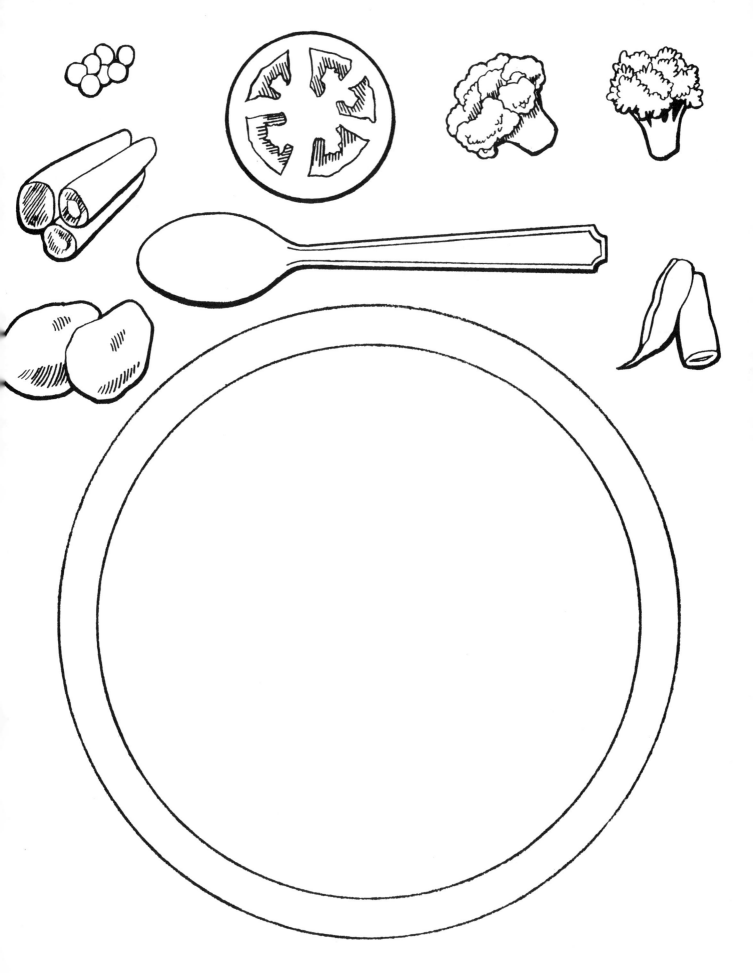

Pattern 4: Eat a Bowl of Soup

11

Grow Some Flowers

God made flowers to add color and beauty to our world. Flower seeds and nectar provide food for bees and other insects. Make a giant sunflower and say thank You to God for the beautiful plants He made.

Materials

Yellow, brown, and green
    construction paper
Sunflower seeds
Paper plate
Glue
Scissors

Directions

1. Use the petal pattern on the next page to cut 12 yellow petals.
2. Use the circle pattern to cut a brown center.
3. Glue petals around the center.
4. Add a stem and leaves cut from green paper.
5. Glue a paper plate behind your sunflower to make it stronger.
6. Glue sunflower seeds in the center. (Chocolate chips or raisins may be substituted.)

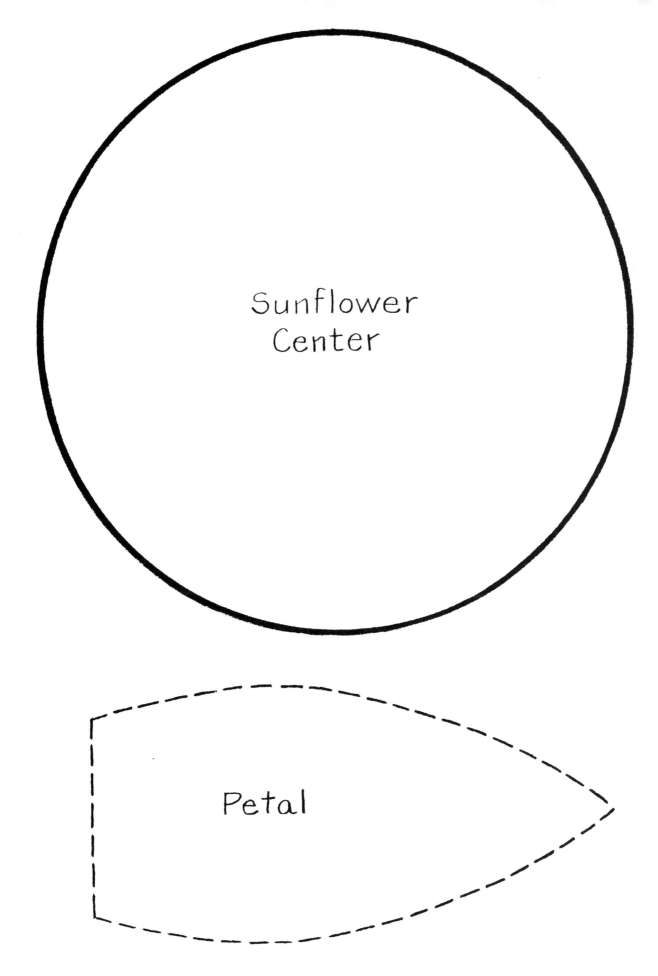

Sunflower
Center

Petal

Pattern 5: Grow Some Flowers **13**

Invite Butterflies to Your Yard

Invite butterflies to your yard by choosing a sunny spot to plant nectar-making flowers such as sweet alyssum, phlox, and chrysanthemums. Thank God for making such beautiful creatures. Then make a paper butterfly.

Materials

Various colors of construction paper
Chenille pipe-cleaner
Scissors
Glue
Tape
Pencil
Straight pin or bulletin board pin

Directions

1. Fold a piece of construction paper in half. Place dotted edge of wing pattern at fold. Trace and cut out wings.
2. Cut out body and glue in center of wings.
3. Use triangle pattern to make colorful construction paper designs. Cut and glue on wings.
4. Bend pipe cleaner to make antennae and tape to butterfly's head.
5. Use a pin to attach butterfly to a pencil. Move gently to make the butterfly fly.

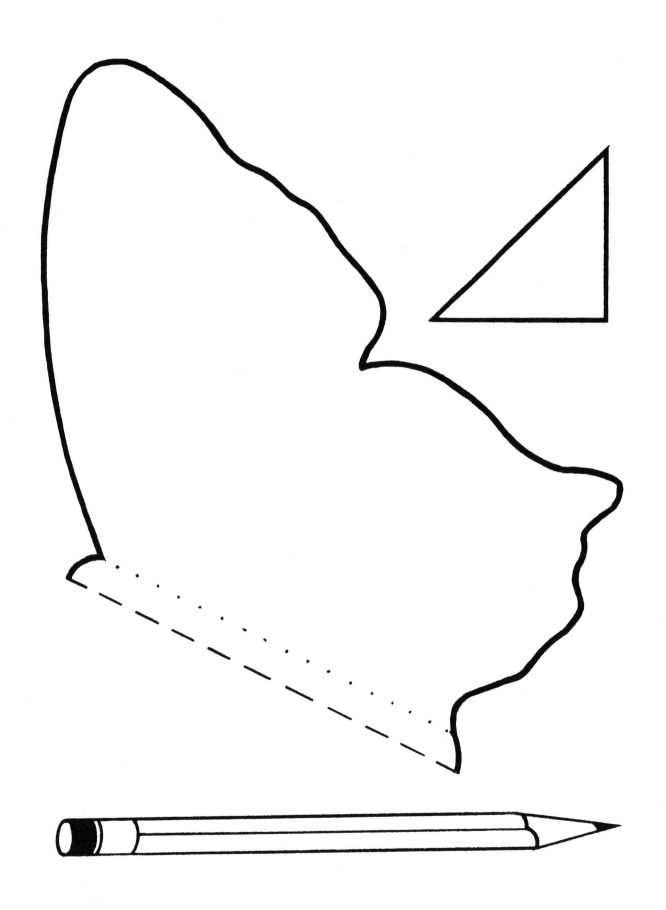

Pattern 6: Invite Butterflies to Your Yard **15**

Start a Compost Pile

God uses "composting" in forests to turn fallen leaves, twigs, and grasses into good food for new plants. Make a compost pile at home. Heap egg shells, coffee grounds, apple cores, potato peels, and other "edible" garbage with grass clippings and leaves. Your garbage will make compost—rich soil to add to your garden. Make a paper wheelbarrow and plan your compost pile.

Materials

Crayons or markers
Construction paper
Scissors
Glue

Directions

1. Color wheelbarrow, cut, and mount on a piece of construction paper.
2. Color pictures. Cut and glue in wheelbarrow.

milk

grass clippings

coffee grounds

leaves

frog

egg shells

Pattern 7: Start a Compost Pile

© CPH 1993

17

Make a Litter Bag

God's colorful world will get messy if we throw our trash on the ground. Make a litter bag to take on your next outing.

Materials

Paper lunch bag
Scissors
Construction paper
Glue
Stapler

Directions

1. Color the picture on the next page. Cut it out and glue to a paper lunch bag.
2. Cut a strip of construction paper and staple it to sides of bag to make a handle.

Pattern 8: Make a Litter Bag

19

Take a Hike in the Woods

9

Take a walk through a wooded area or park and enjoy God's creation. Look for birds, insects, and animals. See if you can find the nests, burrow, or holes where animals live. Talk about what the animals eat and where they find water. Thank God for taking care of His creation.

Materials

Crayons or markers
Pencil

Directions

1. Color the animals on the next page.
2. Draw a line through the maze, naming the animals as you go. (Path may be traced by gluing o-shaped cereal or raisins.)

Picture 9: Take a Hike in the Woods © CPH 1993 **21**

Protect Birds' Nests

10

God planned for mother birds to keep the eggs in their nests warm so baby birds can hatch. If you find a nest with eggs, don't touch them. The mother bird may stay away. Now make a nest that you *can* touch.

Materials

Blue construction paper
Crayons or markers
Scissors
Glue
Paper clip

Directions

1. Color the bird and nest and cut them out.
2. Glue the nest on a half-sheet of blue construction paper.
3. Paper-clip the bird over the nest.

Pattern 10: Protect Birds' Nests   © CPH 1993   **23**

Give Birds Food and Water

God made sure birds know how to find seeds, bugs, and worms to eat and water to drink. You can help take care of birds too. Tie string around orange and lemon peels and unsalted peanuts in shells and hang them from tree branches. Place a shallow container of water in a place where birds will not be harmed by cats. Make a special bird to find out how much God loves you.

Materials

Crayons or markers
Construction paper
Scissors
Glue

Directions

1. Color bird and wing.
2. Cut bird out and glue on construction paper.
3. Cut out wing. Fold up on dotted line and glue to bird, carefully matching the dotted lines. (Cereal or birdseed can be glued on the paper if desired.)
4. Lift the bird's wing to see God's promise to you.

... sold for two pennies? ... of them is forgotten by God.... you are worth more than many sparrows.
Luke 12:6-7

Are not five sparrows sold for two pennies?
Yet not one of them is forgotten by God....
You are worth more than many sparrows.
Luke 12:6-7

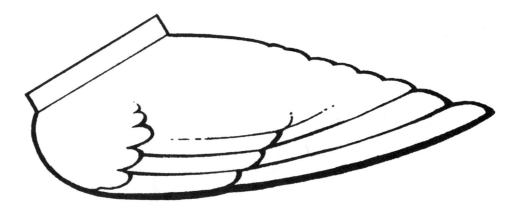

Pattern 11: Give Birds Food and Water **25**

Be Thankful for Worms, Spiders, and Bees

God gives creepy, crawly things important jobs! Worms eat dirt as they burrow through it and leave rich soil behind them. Spiders love to eat insects. Bees travel from flower to flower gathering pollen to make honey. Some of the pollen is dropped on other plants. Then plants can make seeds to grow more plants. Thank God for creating such a good plan. Then put a worm to work in your garden.

Materials

Grocery sack
Construction paper
Scissors
Glue
Crayons or markers

Directions

1. Cut brown paper from a grocery sack. Use crayons or markers to draw a garden scene.
2. Use circle pattern to trace and cut 11 circles from construction paper. Cut one "triangle" tail.
3. Color and cut out the worm's head, or make a head from a circle of construction paper.
4. Glue worm in garden as shown.

**Pattern 12: Be Thankful for Worms,
Spiders, and Bees**

27

Adopt a Beach

Do you live near the ocean, a lake, or a stream? God created cool, blue water to help you relax and enjoy His world. Adopt a small stretch of beach and keep it litter-free. Then finish the picture about a fun day at the beach.

Materials

Blue and tan construction paper
Crayons or markers
Scissors
Glue

Directions

1. Cut a sheet of blue construction paper with a wavy edge to make water. Glue your water to a sheet of tan construction paper to make a beach.
2. Color and cut out the children. Glue them on your picture.
3. Draw sand toys, a sand castle, and sea shells. Cut them out and glue them to your picture.

Pattern 13: Adopt a Beach

29

Leave Tide Pool Animals where They Live

Tide pools provide homes for many tiny sea animals. At some tide pools you may carefully pick up sea animals and put them in a pail of ocean water. Before you leave, gently return them to their tide pool home. Now make a tide pool for some of God's sea creatures.

Materials

Sand paper
Blue construction paper
Crayons or markers
Scissors
Glue

Directions

1. Glue a strip of sand paper to blue construction paper to make a beach.
2. Color and cut out crab and starfish. Glue them to the sandpaper beach.

**Pattern 14. Leave Tide Pool Animals
where They Live**

© CPH 1993

31

Learn about Endangered Species

People, cities, and roads are crowding some of the places God designed for animals to live. Sometimes people kill large numbers of animals. When only a few animals of one type are left, we say those animals are "endangered." Ridley sea turtles are one example of an endangered species. Scientists are helping them find a new place to live. Make a turtle of your own.

Materials

Green construction paper
6-inch paper bowl
Blue construction paper or paper plate
Scissors
Glue
Green tempera paint
Paintbrush

Directions

1. Fold green paper in half. Place turtle pattern on fold. Trace and cut.
2. Glue paper bowl upside down on turtle body.
3. Paint shell (bowl) green.
4. Glue turtle on a paper plate or circle of blue construction paper.

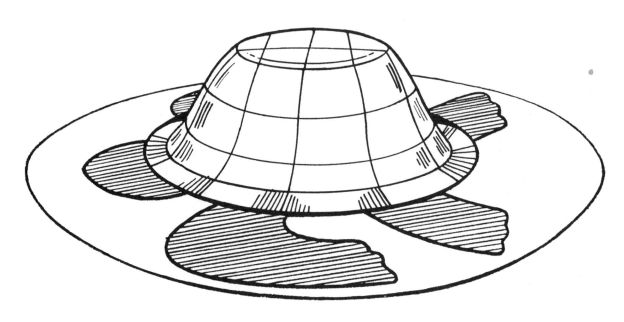

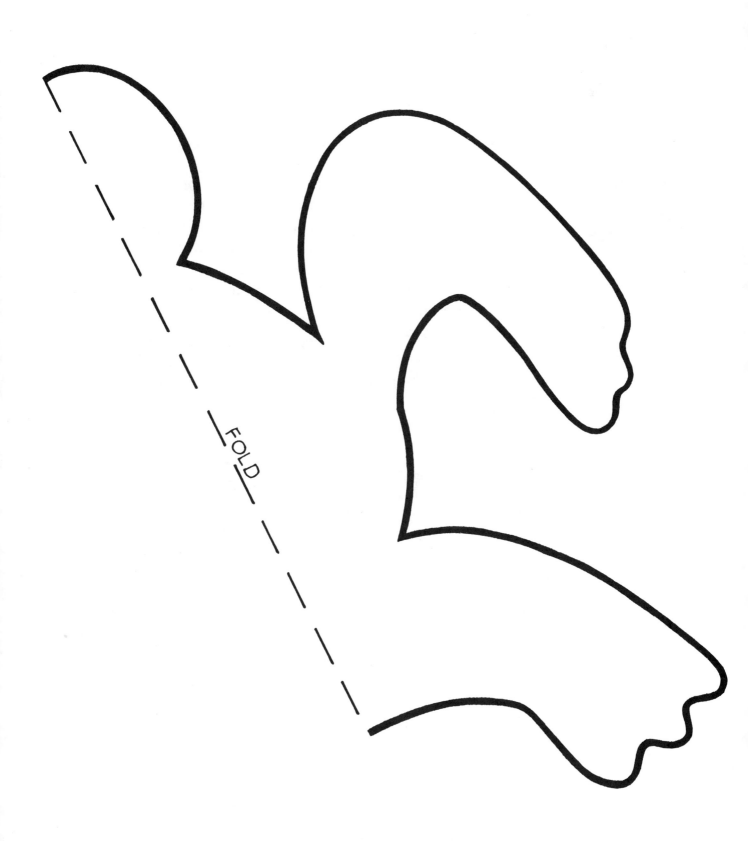

FOLD

Pattern 15. Learn about Endangered Species © CPH 1993 **33**

Read about Rain Forests

16

Rain forests grow near the earth's equator. More kinds of plants and animals can be found in rain forests than in any other place on earth. How many animals can you find in the rain forest on the next page? Color the picture with bright crayons and thank God for creating such a beautiful world. Then you might want to read more about rain forests in a book or encyclopedia.

Picture 16: Read about Rain Forests

© CPH 1993

35

Learn about Whales

Whales are some of the biggest creatures God made. They rise to the ocean's surface to breathe air through a blow hole. The biggest whale, the baleen, can grow to a length of 100 feet and a weight of 150 tons. Hunters used to kill whales to make oil. Now laws protect whales from hunters. Thank God for making these gentle creatures.

Materials

Gray and blue construction paper
Blue mylar strips
Scissors
Glue

Directions

1. Trace whale on gray construction paper and cut it out.
2. Glue whale to blue construction paper.
3. Glue several blue mylar strips spouting up from the whale's blow hole.

Pattern 17: Learn about Whales   © CPH 1993   **37**

Learn about Dolphins

Dolphins are some of the smartest animals God created. They can think ahead and plan what to do. They can learn tricks. They communicate noisily by shifting air between nasal passages inside their heads. Dolphins have helped people in trouble at sea to reach shore safely. Thank God for creating these playful animals.

Connect the dots on the next page. Color the upper half of the dolphin dark gray and the lower part light gray. Read a book or the encyclopedia to find out more about dolphins.

Picture 18: Learn about Dolphins © CPH 1993 **39**

Care about Elephants

It is fun to see elephants at the zoo with their huge bodies, waving trunks, and giant ears. Sometimes elephants are killed so people can sell their tusks for ivory. Ask God to protect these big animals.

Materials

Brown construction paper
White paper
Scissors
Glue

Directions

1. Fold brown construction paper in half. Place pattern for elephant body on fold. Trace and cut.
2. Trace and cut two heads from brown construction paper.
3. Cut two tusks from white paper.
4. Fold ears outward on dotted lines and glue each side of the head to the elephant's body, matching the dotted lines as shown.
5. Glue the tusks on each side of the head.
6. Place elephant's feet two or three inches apart to make it stand.

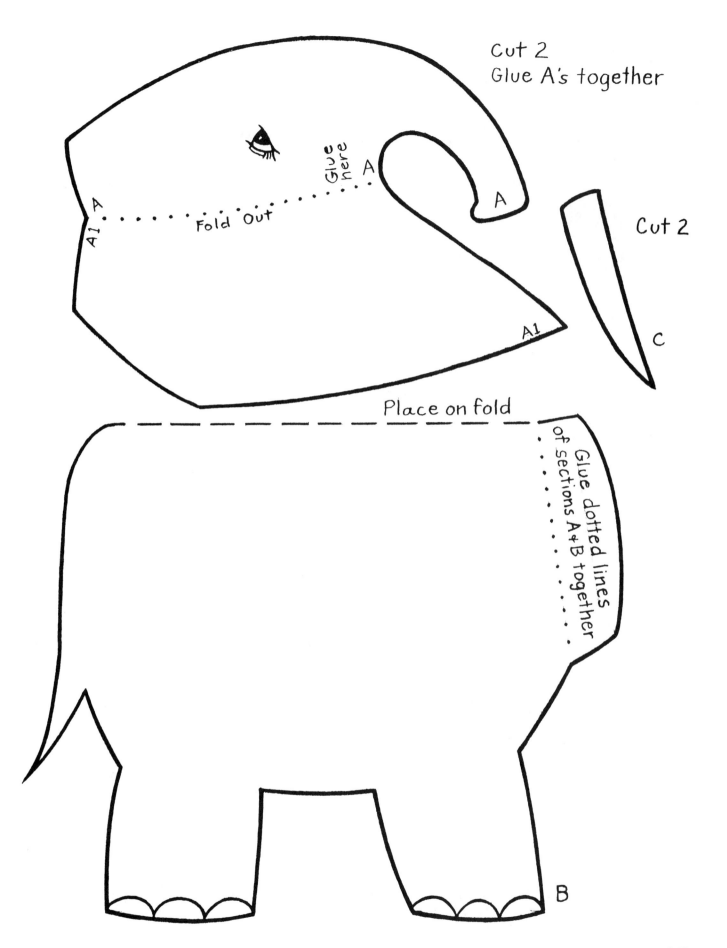

Cut 2
Glue A's together

Cut 2

Pattern 19: Care about Elephants

© CPH 1993

41

Visit a Garden

Have you ever thought about what a wonderful gardener God is? He created trees, bushes, and flowers to grow in spots that are just right for them. You might want to visit an arboretum or botanical garden to see which types of trees and plants grow best where you live.

Look at the plants on the next page. Draw a line from each tree or plant to the place where it grows best on God's earth. Which one lives where there is a lot of water? Which one grows where the weather is hot and dry? Which one grows in high mountains where it gets very cold? Which one grows in warm, moist places?

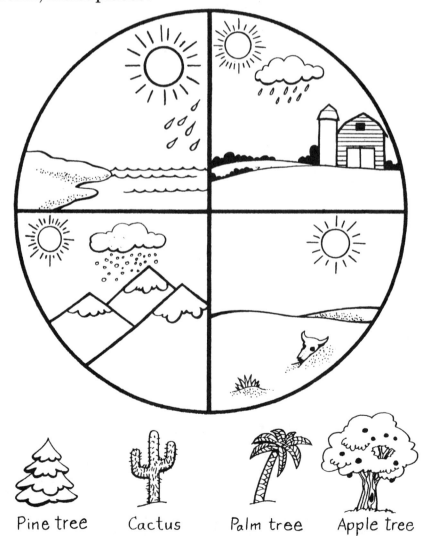

Pine tree   Cactus   Palm tree   Apple tree

Pine tree   Cactus   Palm tree   Apple tree

Picture 20: Visit a Garden   © CPH 1993   **43**

Turn Off the Lights

On the first day of creation, God created light. On the fourth day God made the sun, moon, and stars. During the day, you may not need to turn on lights in the house if enough of God's sunshine comes in the windows. You can save energy by turning off lights when no one is in the room.

Look at the picture of the house on the next page. Draw a happy face by the lights that need to be turned on so people can see to read and work. Draw a sad face by the lights that should be turned off.

Picture 21: Turn Off the Lights

45

22

Tighten Faucets

We need water to live. Plants and animals need water too. You can save a lot of water by turning faucets completely off so they don't drip. Thank God for creating good water.

Materials

Construction paper
Paper-fasteners
Aluminum foil
Scissors
Glue

Directions

1. Cut out picture of sink and glue on a piece of colored construction paper.
2. Cut out faucet handles. Attach to sink, matching dots, with paper-fasteners.
3. Cut a strip of aluminum foil to fit faucet and glue in place.

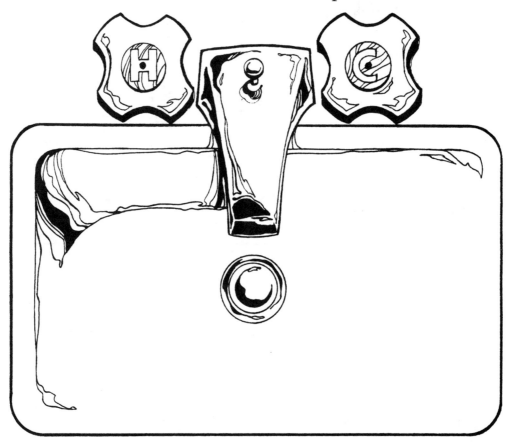

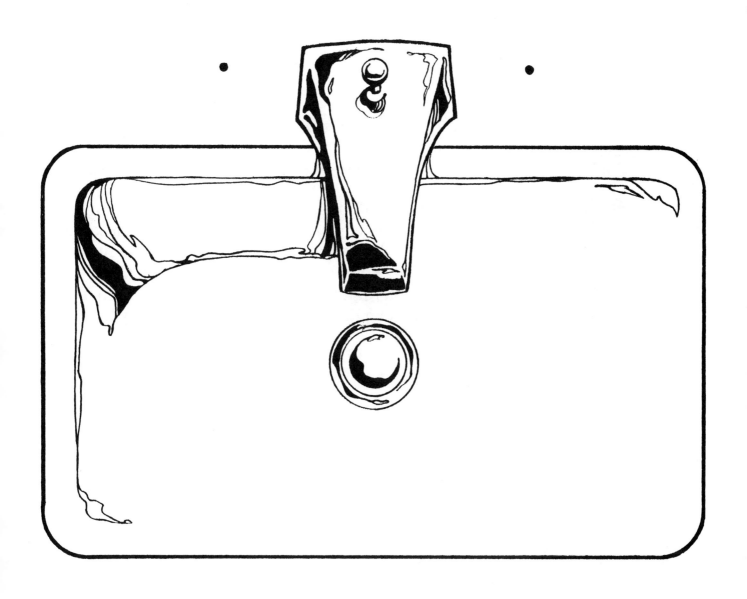

Pattern 22: Tighten Faucets **47**

Hold on to Balloons

It is fun to play with balloons and they make colorful decorations. But sometimes helium balloons are released into the air and sail many miles away. Sometimes animals and birds die when they think the deflated balloons are food and try to eat them. Mylar balloons can lodge in electrical lines and cause power failure. You can help protect God's creation by holding tightly to balloons.

Materials

Yarn or string
Brightly-colored paper, mylar, or
   aluminum foil
Crayons or markers
Glue
Scissors

Directions

1. Color the picture on the next page.
2. Cut and glue a piece of yarn or string from the child's hand to each balloon-shape.
3. Cut and glue colorful balloon shapes in the dotted lines.

Pattern 23: Hold on to Balloons

© CPH 1993

49

Recycle Paper, Aluminum, and Glass

You can help protect God's creation by saving newspapers, aluminum cans, and glass bottles. Picking up litter will keep God's world beautiful. When paper, aluminum, and glass are recycled, they can be used again.

Count the number of recyclable items in each group on the next page. Write the total in the space by each group. Then count the total number of items. See if your family can save that many items in one week!

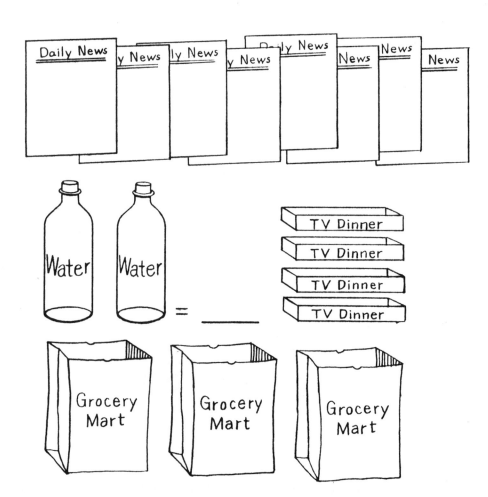

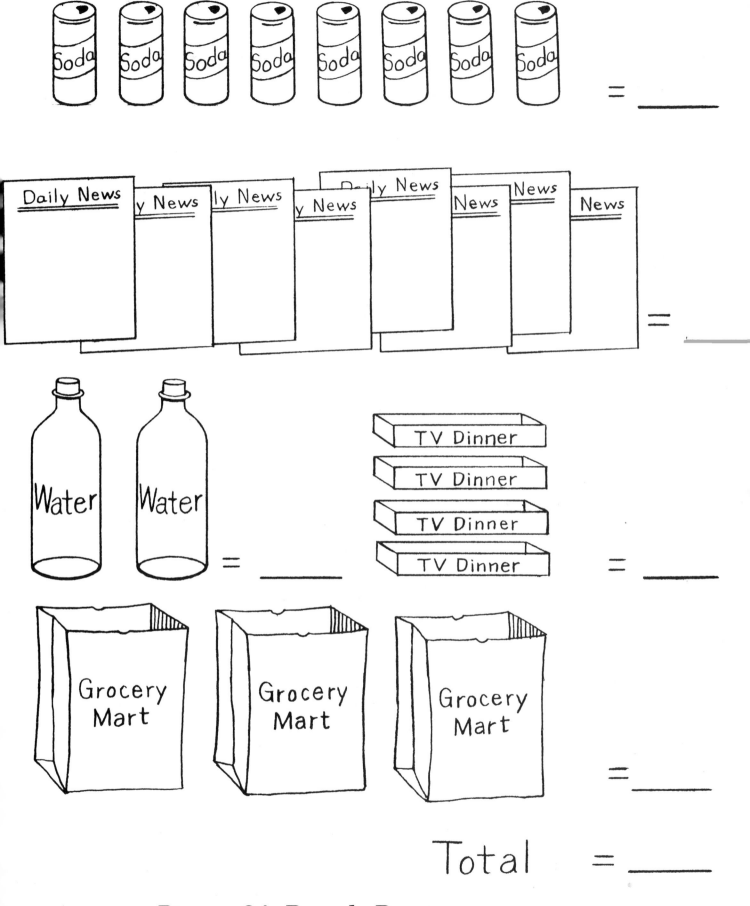

= _____

= _____

Water Water = _____

TV Dinner
TV Dinner
TV Dinner
TV Dinner = _____

Grocery Mart Grocery Mart Grocery Mart = _____

Total = _____

**Picture 24: Recycle Paper,
Aluminum, and Glass**

© CPH 1993

51

Give Away Outgrown Clothes

Don't throw away old clothes that don't fit. You can share God's love by giving your clothes to someone who needs them. And, since it takes energy to produce cotton, run clothing factories, and ship clothing to stores, you will be helping God's earth too.

Materials

Crayons or markers
Scissors
Cardboard
Glue

Directions

1. Color the pictures on the next page.
2. Cut out the figure of the boy and glue it on a piece of cardboard. Trim the cardboard to fit the boy.
3. Carefully cut out the boy's clothes. Bend the tabs to dress the boy in his clothes.

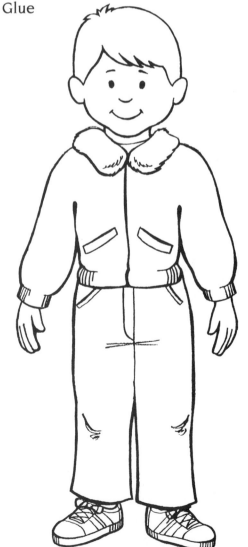

Pattern 53: Give Away Outgrown Clothes © CPH 1993 **53**

Choose Toys That Last

Name your favorite toy. Is it a soft, fuzzy teddy bear? A plastic truck? Some wooden building blocks? A china tea set? Could you keep your favorite toy until you are grown up, and then give the toy to your own child? Choosing toys that last a long time helps protect God's earth. Energy is saved when fewer toys are made. Broken, discarded toys take up less space in landfills. Someday you can tell your children and grandchildren about God's love and give them your favorite toy too!

Materials

Crayons or markers
Scissors
Paper-fasteners
Ribbon
Glue

Directions

1. Color the teddy bear or cut the pieces from brown construction paper.
2. Attach the bear's legs, matching the dots, with paper fasteners.
3. Tie the ribbon in a tiny bow and glue it at the bear's neck.

Pattern 26: Choose Toys That Last © CPH 1993 **55**

Design a Poster

Many times after a rain we can see a rainbow in the sky. We can remember God's promise that He will never again send a flood to cover the whole earth. Thank God for keeping all of His promises—especially His very best promise to send His own Son to die and rise for you. Because of Jesus, you have a new life here on earth and the promise of life in heaven with Him forever.

Use the pictures on the next page to make a poster of God's beautiful creation. You might want to color the picture and hang it up. Or you could cut out the separate pictures and glue them on a background in any way you wish. Add these words to your poster: In the beginning God created the heavens and the earth. Genesis 1:1

Pattern 27: Design a Poster

57

Thank God for His Creation

Read the first chapter of Genesis with your family. Write down some of the beautiful places on God's earth that you like to visit. Tell about your favorite animals and plants. Write a thank-You prayer on the next page, thanking God for making such a beautiful earth. Say the prayer with your family when you go outside or on vacation to enjoy God's creation.

Dear God
Thank You for
making   and   .
I love Your bright   .
        and
In Jesus name, Amen.

Dear God

Thank You for

making   and

I love Your bright

and

In Jesus name, Amen.

Picture 59: Thank God for His Creation © CPH 1993 **59**

Make a Mobile

The colors of the rainbow can help you think of God's beautiful creation and His loving care. Think of red roses and holly berries, yellow buttercups and baby ducklings, green pine trees and tall summer grass, blue sky and ocean waves. Use the pictures on the next page to make a mobile celebrating God's creation.

Materials

Crayons or markers
Scissors
Bright yarn in varying lengths
     from 8- to 24-inches
Tape
Construction paper
Glue
Hanger

Directions

1. Color and cut out the shapes.
2. Tape a piece of yarn to the back of each shape.
3. Trace, cut, and glue a piece of construction paper to the back of each shape to cover the yarn.
4. Tie each piece of yarn to a hanger.

Pattern 29. Make a Mobile © CPH 1993 **61**

Remember God's Gifts

Find some of the things God made in the word puzzle below. You should be able to find: AIR, SUN, RAIN, WATER, PLANTS, ANIMALS, BIRDS, FISH. The words can go across, down, or diagonally. When you are finished, check the answers on page 64.

```
Q  D  O  T  A  Z  I  H  K  U
L  U  M  R  P  K  E  L  O  A
G  F  C  E  M  S  R  A  I  N
W  A  T  E  R  U  W  O  J  I
R  X  A  S  I  T  O  H  C  M
P  L  A  N  T  S  D  A  E  A
M  A  I  S  U  A  U  E  W  L
B  I  R  D  S  I  N  N  O  S
U  S  D  A  T  M  F  I  S  H
W  A  M  O  D  L  R  C  B  P
```

Draw a Picture of God's Creation

What is your favorite spot on God's earth? Draw a picture of that place. Then close your eyes and pretend you are sitting there. Thank God for creating such a beautiful place for you here on earth, and for preparing a wonderful home for you in heaven.

My Favorite Spot in God's Creation

Q D O T A Z I H K U

L U M R P K E L O A

G F C E M S R A I N

W A T E R U W O J I

R X A S I T O H C M

P L A N T S D A E A

M A I S U A U E W L

B I R D S I N O S

U S D A T M F I S H

W A M O D L R C B P

© CPH 1993 **Answers for word puzzle, page 62**